KIM JONG UN

KIM JONG UN

Secretive North Korean Leader

JON M. FISHMAN

LERNER PUBLICATIONS ◆ MINNEAPOLIS

Lerner Publications Company
A division of Lerner Publishing Group, Inc.
241 First Avenue North
Minneapolis, MN 55401 USA

For reading levels and more information, look up this title at www.lernerbooks.com.

Image credits: Getty Images, p. 2; Korea Summit Press Pool/AFP/Getty Images, p. 6; Saul Loeb/ AFP/Getty Images, pp. 8, 9; Eric Lafforgue/Gamma-Rapho/Getty Images, p. 10; Laura Westlund/ Independent Picture Service, p. 11; Bibliothèque Nationale de France, p. 13; Heritage Images/ Getty Images, p. 14; Universal History Archive/UIG/Getty Images, p. 15; Bettmann/Getty Images, pp. 16, 17; Hulton Deutsch/Corbis/Getty Images, p. 18; Ian Timberlake/AFP/Getty Images, p. 19; Anthony Asael/Art in All of Us/Getty Images, p. 20; Kyodo News/Getty Images, pp. 21, 33, 35; STR/EPN/Newscom, p. 23; Robyn Beck/AFP/Getty Images, p. 24; AFP/Getty Images, p. 25; Gerhard Joren/LightRocket/Getty Images, p. 26; Karen Bleier/AFP/Getty Images, p. 29; Tengku Bahar/AFP/Getty Images, p. 31; KCNA/AFP/Getty Images, p. 32; Corbis/Getty Images, p. 34 (left); Eric Lafforgue/Art in All of Us/Corbis News/Getty Images, p. 34 (right); STR/AFP/Getty Images, p. 36; Woohae Cho/AFP/Getty Images, p. 37; KNS/AFP/Getty Images, p. 38; Handout/ South Korean Defence Ministry/Getty Images, p. 39; Official White House photo by Shealah Craighead, p. 40.

Cover: STR/AFP/Getty Images.

Library of Congress Cataloging-in-Publication Data

The Cataloging-in-Publication Data for *Kim Jong Un: Secretive North Korean Leader* is on file at the Library of Congress.
ISBN 978-1-5415-3919-8 (lib. bdg.)
ISBN 978-1-5415-4349-2 (eb pdf)

Manufactured in the United States of America
1-45102-35929-9/20/2018

CONTENTS

Kim Jong Un, leader of North Korea, in April 2018

Something historic was about to happen at Capella Resort on Sentosa Island in Singapore. It was June 12, 2018, and reporters from around the world had gathered at the luxury hotel to capture images of an amazing meeting. A red carpet stretched across the walkway in front of them. Behind the carpet stood a row of flags. Half of the flags represented the United States. The others represented the Democratic People's Republic of Korea, known to most as North Korea.

Two men approached the center of the walkway from opposite directions. A buzz filled the air as cameras clicked and whirred to catch every moment. From the right strolled US president Donald Trump. From the left came Kim Jong Un, leader of North Korea. The men extended their right arms as they walked, meeting in the middle to shake hands. North Korea and the United States shared a long and turbulent history, and the leaders of the nations had never before met face-to-face.

North Korea sits on the northern half of the Korean

peninsula, an area that has been a hot spot for conflict for thousands of years. Located between China, Russia, and Japan, the peninsula is in one of the world's most densely populated regions. North Korea became a country just after World War II (1939–1945), and it has been at odds with the United States ever since. All-out war between the countries in the 1950s led to a cold war, or period of disagreement without military fighting, in the 1960s and 1970s. In the 1980s, the conflict continued, focusing on North Korea's pursuit of weapons of mass destruction. When Trump and Kim met in 2018, North Korea's nuclear weapons program was the main reason.

The two leaders gripped hands and looked each other

Kim shakes hands with Trump at their historic meeting in June 2018.

Kim and Trump sit down with their delegates at the summit in Singapore.

in the eye for exactly thirteen seconds. They turned and faced the cameras before exiting together to the left. Then Kim and Trump, along with two translators, met alone for almost an hour. After the private meeting, the two leaders and their aides had a working lunch.

To close the summit, Trump and Kim signed a document called a joint statement. It summarized their discussions and laid out a plan for future talks. The leaders stated their desire for a more positive relationship between the two countries and peace on the Korean peninsula. Kim also agreed to work toward removing nuclear weapons from the Korean peninsula.

After returning to the United States, Trump posted a

message on Twitter. "Just landed—a long trip, but everybody can now feel much safer than the day I took office," he wrote. "There is no longer a Nuclear Threat from North Korea." The statement surprised many people in the United States and elsewhere. North Korea had a history of not living up to its promises about nuclear weapons, and the joint statement Kim Jong Un signed in June was just another promise. He is the third member of his family to control North Korea as its absolute leader. Over the generations, the Kim family has held on to power by any means necessary. Since taking over as the country's dictator in 2011, Kim Jong Un has proven that like his father and grandfather before him, he's willing to do whatever it takes to keep his position.

War and Conquest

North Korea is a secretive country. The government withholds so much information from the public that Kim Jong Un's birth date is a mystery. He was born in North Korea in the early 1980s, probably on January 8. The story of Kim's life intertwines with the history of the country he rules.

Late in the nineteenth century, the areas that would become North Korea and South Korea united under the Joseon dynasty. But external forces threatened to plunge the region into turmoil. Two of Korea's powerful neighbors, China and Japan, wanted to increase their influence on the Korean peninsula. The two countries moved troops into the region, and war broke out between them in 1894. China expected its enormous military force to provide an advantage, but Japan had more advanced military technology and won the war. China asked for peace in 1895. Japan's victory gave the country control over large portions of Korean territory, including part of the country's coal and iron resources.

Russia also had its eye on Korea. In 1896 Russia and

Korean Peninsula and Surrounding Areas

China agreed to an alliance that would resist Japanese power on the Korean peninsula. Russia moved military forces into the region, and Japan decided to attack to protect its interests. Fighting on February 8, 1904, sparked the Russo-Japanese War. With a supply advantage and soldiers who were used to fighting in the area, Japan won the war in 1905. The victory gave Japan complete control over the peninsula—Korea became a Japanese colony in 1910.

Over the next several decades, the Japanese colonial government waged a campaign to erase Korean language and culture from the peninsula. They demanded that people speak Japanese in public places such as schools. Officials required many Koreans to take Japanese names. Buildings in Japanese styles sprang up around the country to house hundreds of thousands of Japanese newcomers. Meanwhile, colonial officials destroyed historic Korean buildings or turned them into tourist attractions. Officials imprisoned, tortured, and killed Koreans they saw as enemies of Japan.

Many Koreans resisted Japan's brutal control of their country. On March 1, 1919, local Korean leaders started a huge protest movement. The leaders read a statement in public in Seoul, the capital city, declaring Korea's independence from Japan. Others read the same statement in towns across the country. The March First Movement protests inspired millions of Koreans to demonstrate against Japanese rule. Japanese officials responded to the marches, speeches, and strikes with violence. They killed and arrested thousands of protesters across the nation.

The March First Movement marked the beginning of a decades-long struggle against Japan's control of Korea. Besides protests, some Koreans fought back with violence. Japan's occupation of the peninsula forced many Koreans north into Manchuria, a region in present-day China. From there, Korean guerrilla groups launched assaults against Japanese forces. Guerrillas use tactics such as surprise attacks and sabotage but are not part of a formal military. One of the guerrillas in Manchuria in the 1930s was Kim Il Sung, a dedicated fighter and Kim Jong Un's grandfather. Kim Il Sung had moved with his family to Manchuria in 1920.

Korean protesters demonstrate against Japan's rule in Seoul in March 1919.

The Soviet Union

For hundreds of years, czars controlled Russia. These monarchs had complete power and authority. Early in the twentieth century, a series of revolutions and conflicts changed Russia's political landscape and ended the rule of the czars. In 1922 Russia and some neighboring countries joined to form the Soviet Union. Vladimir Lenin, who started the Russian Communist Party, led the new country.

Lenin and his fellow Communists believed the public, represented by a strong government, should control the Soviet Union's resources and factories. The government controlled industries such as mining and banking and divided resources among the people as needed. Private ownership was limited. Lenin died in 1924, and the general secretary of the country's Communist Party, Joseph Stalin, became the country's new leader. By the early 1930s, Stalin had secured his position as the nation's dictator. His government commanded almost every aspect of the country's industries and resources. The Soviet Union dissolved in 1991 and broke into twelve independent republics.

Vladimir Lenin (*left*) and Joseph Stalin in 1922

Kim Il Sung as a young man

News of changes in Russia and the beginning of the Soviet Union in the 1920s brought a sense of hope to some of the region's troubled people. Communism, which promised to divide a country's wealth evenly among all citizens, sounded good to many Koreans who lived as second-class citizens or had fled their own country. In the 1930s, Kim Il Sung joined the local Communist Party. He also joined guerrilla groups and quickly became a leader in both politics and warfare. In one daring raid, Kim led a group of guerrilla fighters into northern Korea. They briefly drove away the local Japanese forces before retreating.

As Kim Il Sung's reputation rose as a resistance fighter and a Communist Party member, Japan sought to expand its empire in the Pacific Ocean. On December 7, 1941, a Japanese fighting force with dozens of warships and airplanes approached the US military base at Pearl Harbor, Hawaii. With no warning, the planes bombed Pearl Harbor, killing more than two thousand. The next day, President Franklin Roosevelt spoke to the American people. "The attack yesterday on the Hawaiian Islands has caused severe damage to American naval and military forces," he said. "I regret to tell you that very many American lives have been lost." The US declared war on Japan and entered World War II hours after Roosevelt's speech.

The war eventually ended in victory for the United States and its allies, including the Soviet Union. Their success ended a generation of Japanese rule in Korea and gave control of the region to the United States and the Soviet Union. Yet again, foreign powers would dictate the fate of the Korean people.

Battleships at Pearl Harbor burn after Japan bombed the military base there.

Roosevelt signs a declaration of war against Japan on December 8, 1941.

The Kim Dynasty

Who would lead Korea? After decades of struggle against Japanese control, what form of government would the people accept? The United States, which controlled the southern half of the peninsula, and the Soviets in the North couldn't agree on this. In 1948 the United States set up a government in South Korea and named Syngman Rhee president. The US planned for the South Korean people to choose future leaders in democratic elections. The Soviet Union responded by elevating Kim Il Sung, who had formed a Communist Party called the Korean Workers' Party (WKP) two years earlier, to lead North

Korea. Both countries claimed authority over the entire peninsula.

Violence soon followed. Brief military flare-ups along the North-South border had blossomed into full-scale war by 1950. On June 25, Kim ordered the Soviet-backed North Korean army to invade South Korea. The United States sent military forces to support South Korea, and the Korean War (1950–1953) began. Over the next several years, millions of people died in the fighting. In 1953 the two sides agreed to a cease-fire. The agreement didn't officially end the war, but it brought peace to the

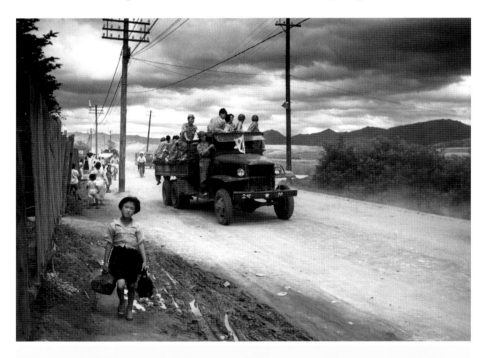

South Korean soldiers drive past civilians during the Korean War.

This symbol of the WKP has three parts, showing three kinds of people in the country. The hammer stands for industrial workers, the calligraphy brush represents educated people, and the sickle stands for peasants.

area. The border between North Korea and South Korea remained mostly unchanged, and Kim Il Sung still ruled in the North.

Peace allowed Kim to turn his attention toward securing his place as North Korea's leader. After decades of outside influence on the Korean peninsula, Kim's vision for his country was one of fierce independence. His political philosophy, *juche*, meant "self-reliance." In the years after the Korean War, he severed contact with many nations, especially the United States and other Western countries. The Communist government placed restrictions on travel into and out of North Korea. It tightly controlled the media. The government took charge of the country's agriculture, industry, and almost all private property.

Kim taught his people that *juche* referred to national

North Koreans bow before a statue of Kim Il Sung in 2008.

rather than individual self-reliance. All personal wants and needs were secondary to the needs of the country. By giving everything to the nation, the North Korean people would share in the collective success of their great country and leader. In this way, loyalty to the government became like a religion in North Korea, and Kim Il Sung became its godlike leader.

Kim's strict policy of isolation created hardships for the North Korean people. The country struggled to grow enough food, resulting in periods of famine. Officials who spoke out against Kim's policies risked their jobs and even their lives. In events called purges, he fired groups of people from their jobs and their roles in the WKP. He often expelled them from the country. Many of those Kim saw as enemies of the state were arrested. Government agents tortured and killed other purge victims.

No matter what was happening in the country, the government-run media presented a flattering image of its ruler. Images of Kim Il Sung, known as Great Leader, seemed to be everywhere in North Korea during his decades in power. Statues and murals glorified him. Government propaganda told tales of Kim's heroic deeds against invaders of the Korean peninsula.

Family Business

For decades Kim Il Sung groomed his son, Kim Jong Il, to take over as leader of North Korea. Kim Jong Il had three sons and two daughters. He was especially fond of Jong Un. He felt that he shared a similar personality with his youngest son. Before Jong Il even became the leader of North Korea, he decided that Jong Un would be his heir. At his eighth birthday party, Jong Un wore a North Korean general's uniform. Some of North Korea's top military officials attended the party, and they bowed to the boy. That day was the first hint that Jong Un could someday become the country's leader.

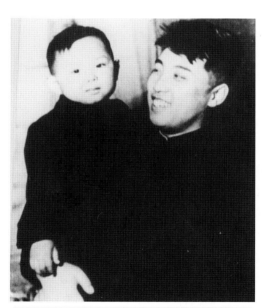

Kim Il Sung (*right*) holds his young son, Kim Jong Il.

21

Ko Yong Hui

Like many parts of Kim Jong Un's life, most details about his mother—Ko Yong Hui—are a mystery. Records show that Ko Yong Hui was born in Osaka, Japan, in 1952. She moved to North Korea in the early 1960s. Later, she joined the Mansudae Art Troupe, a group of dancers and musicians. Ko traveled to Japan in 1973 to perform as one of the group's top dancers.

Ko's relationship with Kim Jong Il began in 1976. Kim already had two children from previous relationships. Ko and Kim had three children together: Jong Chul, Jong Un, and Yo Jong. Ko attended official events and had political influence with the country's leaders, including Kim. She died in 2004.

Kim Il Sung's line of succession was in place, but he wasn't ready to give up power just yet. He began building nuclear weapons to help secure North Korea from foreign threats, mainly South Korea and the United States. Nuclear weapons have incredible destructive power. Their presence on the Korean peninsula would have been especially troubling, since North Korea and South Korea were technically still at war. In 1985 North Korea signed an international agreement called the Nuclear Nonproliferation Treaty. The agreement prevented the country from building nuclear weapons. But in 1993, the North Korean government refused to allow outside inspectors to look at certain nuclear sites in the country. Pressure mounted on North Korea to prove it was not building weapons in secret.

As nuclear tensions rose, young Jong Un lived a life of luxury. Chefs prepared his meals. He vacationed with his family in Europe and Japan. They traveled back and forth from their house on the beach to their main home in Pyongyang, North Korea's capital. In Pyongyang, Jong Un could spend time in their home movie theater, but he preferred to play basketball. "He started playing basketball, and he became obsessed with it," said his aunt, Ko Yong Suk. "He used to sleep . . . with his basketball." He was a huge fan of the Chicago Bulls. The government had banned foreign TV and radio broadcasts in the country for all but the ruling elite, so many North Koreans didn't even know the Bulls existed.

An undated photo of a young Kim Jong Un

On July 8, 1994, Kim Il Sung died after more than forty-five years as North Korea's Great Leader. As Kim Il Sung had wished, Kim Jong Il assumed power. His people called him Dear Leader, and he continued his father's policies. The country stayed isolated. Like his father, Kim demanded complete loyalty to himself and the nation. The birthdays of Great Leader and Dear Leader became the country's most important holidays. North Koreans were required to wear loyalty badges that showed portraits of the Kims, and children learned about their leaders' heroic deeds in school. The country's religious devotion to the Kim family continued.

In October the United States and North Korea signed a deal called the Agreed Framework. North Korea promised to end its nuclear weapons program in exchange for peaceful energy technology, oil, and other resources. It was a promise the country didn't keep.

North Korean loyalty badges showing Kim Jong Il (*left*) and Kim Il Sung

A government-run farm in Kaesong, North Korea, in April 2007

Hunger

North Korea wasn't as self-reliant as it aspired to be. Cheap imports of fuel and chemicals from the Soviet Union helped North Korean farmers keep up with the nation's demand for food. But those imports ended when the Soviet Union broke apart in 1991. In the mid-1990s, food shortages struck North Korea and caused widespread suffering and death.

North Korea's short rice-growing season lasts from May to October. With mountains covering much of the country, only about 20 percent of the land is arable, or good for growing crops. For decades, the nation's farmers had struggled to produce enough food for the country. To increase arable land, some farmers cut down forests and planted crops on the sides of hills. Beginning in 1995, a series of droughts followed by heavy rains led to flooding. With fewer forests to guard against erosion, many farms were ruined. Food production sank, and hunger spread.

Kim Jong Il's government did a poor job of distributing what little food the country produced. To protect Kim's hold on power, more food went to military and Communist Party members than to other people. Other countries and organizations sent food aid, but North Korean government officials were in charge of distributing it. Often the food didn't go to those who needed it most. Some experts believe that millions of

A woman walks past storage cellars near Mount Myohyang, North Korea, in the early 1990s. Dry ground and dead trees became signs of drought in the country during this time.

North Koreans died of hunger between 1995 and 1998. During most of this time, Kim Jong Un was attending boarding school in Switzerland.

As his people starved, Kim Jong Il pushed ahead with new weapons programs that he hoped would protect North Korea from its enemies. In 1998 the military launched a Taepodong-1 missile. It sailed over Japan before landing in the Pacific Ocean. Missiles like the Taepodong-1 were capable of carrying nuclear weapons, and many people believed that North Korea had never abandoned its nuclear program. Yet experts weren't sure if North Korea possessed the technology to make a nuclear device small enough for the Taepodong-1 to carry. Japan and other nations considered the missile a threat and condemned the launch.

On January 29, 2002, US president George W. Bush delivered the State of the Union address. Bush suggested that North Korea and some other countries were part of an "axis of evil." He said, "North Korea is a regime arming with missiles and weapons of mass destruction, while starving its citizens." Later in 2002, the US government said that North Korea had admitted to running a nuclear weapons program for the past several years. The Agreed Framework of 1994, North Korea's promise not to build nuclear weapons, was void.

North Korea ramped up its nuclear program after Bush's speech, and Kim Jong Un prepared himself to run it. After a few years in Switzerland, he returned and studied physics at Kim Il Sung University in Pyongyang.

In 2002 he began training at Kim Il Sung Military Academy to become an officer in the North Korean armed forces.

Nuclear Power

At meetings in Beijing, China, in April 2003, a North Korean official told US agents that the country had built at least one nuclear weapon. The official then hinted that North Korea might test a nuclear device in the near future. Some observers believed that such threats were an attempt by North Korea to distract people from problems at home. Modern technology such as cell phones and the internet made it harder for the government to contain information. The world was finding out more and more about the problems in North Korea.

More than 25 percent of North Koreans lived in poverty. Getting enough to eat was a constant problem for everyone but top government officials and their favored people. Under such circumstances, devotion to the nation wasn't enough to keep everyone in line. Kim Jong Il resorted to fear. He oversaw a system of prison camps called *kwanliso*, where he detained anyone he saw as an enemy. Prisoners faced hard labor, torture, and death. *Kwanliso* camps held tens of thousands of political prisoners at a time. The harsh conditions in North Korea caused many people to attempt to flee the country. Kim tightened security at the borders and threw those

Human rights organizations have publicly protested the way the North Korean government treats its citizens.

he caught into *kwanliso* camps.

In October 2006, the North Korean military declared that they had successfully tested a nuclear weapon for the first time. US director of national intelligence John Negroponte reported that air samples from the Korean peninsula contained "debris consistent with a North Korea nuclear test." The United Nations, an international group dedicated to world peace, imposed sanctions, or economic punishments aimed at a nation, on the country. These sanctions included bans on certain types of trade and travel. The United Nations also banned the trade of some luxury goods into North Korea, a direct strike at the Kim family's lush lifestyle.

Kim Jong Un graduated from the military academy not long after his country became a nuclear power. He soon began attending official events, including military inspections, at his father's side. However, Kim Jong Un's brother, Kim Jong Chul, also attended such events.

Outside observers still weren't sure which of Kim's sons would someday take over as leader.

That changed in September 2010, when Kim Jong Un became a four-star general in the North Korean military. A month later, he became second-in-command behind

Trade with China

After the demise of the Soviet Union in 1991, China stepped in as North Korea's biggest ally and most important trading partner. China supported sanctions against North Korea after nuclear tensions around 2006, but more than 90 percent of North Korea's international trade remained with China. North Korea's neighbor provides the isolated nation with food and most of its fuel resources.

More recently, China has said it doesn't want North Korea to continue building nuclear weapons and threatening its neighbors with missile tests. China favors stability in the region. If North Korea begins a war, it would be close enough to affect China, even if the country isn't directly involved. And some experts say that China, as one of the most powerful countries in the area, would not hesitate to enter a potential conflict, with the goal of maintaining or even gaining strength in the region.

Many Asian newspapers ran headlines about North Korea's nuclear testing in October 2006.

Kim Jong Il on the Central Military Commission, one of the Communist Party's most important groups. With his brother nowhere in sight, Kim Jong Un stood next to his father at a military parade to celebrate the sixty-fifth anniversary of the WKP. The government had sent a clear message to the world: Kim Jong Un would be the next leader of North Korea.

North Korean citizens mourn Kim Jong Il in Pyongyang.

Supreme Leader

North Korea's state-run media made an earth-shattering announcement on December 19, 2011. Kim Jong Il, Dear Leader, was dead. He had had a heart attack two days earlier. The news sent shock waves through the country. As the information trickled beyond the borders, people around the world wondered what would happen next. Would power transfer peacefully to Kim Jong Un?

In North Korea, soldiers collapsed in grief. Children wailed. Men and women tore at their hair and shouted at the sky. Dear Leader was gone! North Koreans across the country gathered to mourn the man they had worshipped. Yet some outside observers questioned the sincerity of the emotions. After the hardship and fear of the past two decades, maybe people were just doing what they thought government officials expected.

Kim Jong Il had made it clear that his youngest son was his heir, but now Kim Jong Un and his supporters had to convince the North Korean people that he was up to the job. He wasn't yet thirty years old, making him the youngest leader of a country in the world. His early life had been so secretive that no one knew much about him.

Kim Jong Il had convinced many of his closest advisers to support Kim Jong Un's rise to power. Jong Un's uncle, Jang Song Thaek, and aunt, Kim Kyong Hui, were powerful members of the North Korean government. The young leader would likely lean on his relatives for advice and support. Kim Jong Un also needed top officials in the military and Communist Party to support him. On December 31, the WKP made it official. They named Jong Un supreme commander of the armed forces. At the time, North Korea had the fourth-largest army in the world.

Kim Jong Un in 2012

The North Korean government began a propaganda campaign designed to endear Kim Jong Un to the country. State media called him "supreme leader of the WKP, state, and army." It aired interviews with people who seemed thrilled about their new leader.

"We will absolutely entrust our destiny to General Kim Jong Un," North Korean factory manager Pak Song Chol said. Kim Jong Un tried to link himself to the godlike legacy of Kim Il Sung. He copied his grandfather's haircut, clothing style, and laugh. He learned his grandfather's gestures and movements. Some people say Kim Jong Un even gained weight to look more like Kim Il Sung.

After becoming North Korea's supreme leader, Kim Jong Un (*right*) began to dress and behave like his grandfather, Kim Il Sung (*left*).

Kim Jong Un (*right*) with army chief Ri Yong Ho at an event celebrating the seventieth birthday of Kim Jong Il in 2012

Kim Jong Il had been an intensely private man. In his years in office, he gave just one known public speech in North Korea, and it lasted about ten seconds. On April 15, 2012, Kim Jong Un showed his people that he would have a different style. He spoke before thousands in Pyongyang as part of celebrations for his grandfather, who would have turned one hundred years old that day. The style was different, but the substance remained the same. Kim Jong Un made it clear that he approved of his father's aggressive military policies. "We have to make every effort to reinforce the people's armed forces," he said. The event included a military parade that showcased thousands of soldiers and technology, including a display of huge missiles.

Kim Jong Un and his wife, Ri Sol Ju

Around this time, a young woman appeared with Kim at some official events. No one knew who she was. North Korea's previous leaders had barely acknowledged their wives in public. Could the young woman be an unknown sister?

In July 2012, North Korean state media announced that Kim had married Ri Sol Ju. Ri was born in Chongjin, North Korea, in the early 1980s and attended Kim Il Sung University. In 2005 she traveled to South Korea as part of a cheering squad for the Asian Athletics Championships. How the couple met is unknown, but South Korean officials believe they had already been married for three years when North Korea made the official wedding announcement in 2012. They have three children born between 2010 and 2017.

A New Beginning?

"Traitor Jang Song Thaek Executed," read North Korean state media's shocking headline in December 2013, making news around the world. Kim Jong Un's uncle had been a member of the WKP since the 1970s. Jang's marriage to Kim Il Sung's sister had helped him rise in the party quickly, and many thought Kim Jong Un had relied on his uncle for guidance since taking power. The young dictator proved them wrong. Officials accused Jang of trying to overthrow the government, sentenced him to death, and immediately shot him. Kim was following his father's footsteps by purging people such as Jang who posed a threat to his hold on power, and he wasn't finished yet. More purges followed. Kim's older brother, Kim Jong Nam, was later assassinated in an airport in Malaysia.

Kim also continued *kwanliso*. The system of prison camps may be the government's most effective way to instill fear in its people. North Korea imprisons hundreds of thousands of men, women, and children in such camps,

South Korean television news showed footage of Jang Song Thaek's court trial before his execution in December 2013.

often without trials. Many people in *kwanliso* haven't even committed a crime but are punished for something done by a family member. Torture, rape, and public executions are common in the camps.

Like North Korea's previous leaders, Kim thought nuclear weapons could prevent invasions from foreign countries. The nation's first nuclear weapons test with Kim as leader took place in 2013. In a statement announcing the test, North Korean officials called the United States "the sworn enemy of the Korean people." US president Barack Obama said North Korea's actions threatened peace in the region. The United Nations punished the country with sanctions.

North Korea held a huge military rally at Kim Il Sung Square in Pyongyang on September 13, 2016, to celebrate its nuclear weapons testing.

This North Korean military drone crashed into a mountain in Samcheok, South Korea, in early 2014.

The standoff led to more tests and threats. Early in 2016, Kim's government set off its biggest nuclear explosion yet in an underground testing area. North Korea said it was a hydrogen bomb, a weapon with more destructive power than any device previously tested by the country. Meanwhile, the country kept building and testing missiles that could soar farther and farther. They also claimed to have nuclear weapons small enough to attach to the missiles. The United Nations imposed more sanctions, but it was difficult to punish the North Korean government without increasing the suffering of its people.

In January 2017, Donald Trump became president of the United States. Previous presidents had careful responses to North Korean weapons tests, wary of saying anything that might provoke violence. Trump had a

Trump receives a letter from Kim Jong Un in June 2018.

different plan. In July Kim's military tested a missile that they said could strike anywhere in the world. State-run media said that if the United States attempted to remove Kim from power, the military wouldn't hesitate to launch a nuclear strike against the country.

Trump spoke to reporters about the incident from a golf course in New Jersey. With his arms crossed in front of him, he warned North Korea not to threaten the United States. "They will be met with fire and fury like the world has never seen," Trump said. Trump later called Kim "Little Rocket Man."

Kim responded by referring to Trump as "dotard," or a person who has lost mental sharpness with age.

Many people thought that war was about to begin on the Korean peninsula. When world leaders spoke to each other the way Kim and Trump had, the result was usually violence. Rumors swirled in spring 2018, and countries in the region geared up for war. Then a series of meetings took place between officials from South Korea, North Korea, and the United States. They chose June 12 for a historic meeting between the leaders of the United States and North Korea.

No North Korean leader had flown outside of the country in thirty-two years. With tensions high and trust fragile between the two sides, the North Korean government arranged for three planes to travel with Kim to the summit in Singapore. That way, Kim's enemies wouldn't know which plane he was on. Kim also brought a bulletproof limousine and a personal toilet on the trip, as he does whenever he travels. Human waste contains information about a person's health. As always, the North Korean government held its secrets tightly.

People had a wide range of reactions to the Trump-Kim summit. In the United States, many took a wait-and-see attitude. The summit was a good start, but North Korea had backed out of promises to disarm in the past. In North Korea, people spoke cautiously of the summit and wished their supreme leader well. Many South Koreans were ecstatic at the prospect of peace in the region and better relations with their neighbors to the north.

Whether it was Trump's fiery style or North Korea's advancing nuclear technology that drove the sides to talk, the meeting in Singapore was just a first step. North Korea may have up to sixty nuclear weapons and hundreds of missiles capable of striking beyond their borders. It would take years to dismantle such a weapons program.

As the supreme leader of North Korea, Kim Jong Un alone will decide to abandon his nuclear weapons and open the country to the world or continue to let his people suffer in isolation.

IMPORTANT DATES

1895   Victory in the First Sino-Japanese War gives Japan influence on the Korean peninsula.

1910   Korea becomes a Japanese colony.

1919   Organized protests on March 1 start the March First Movement against Japanese control of Korea.

1920   Kim Il Sung moves to Manchuria with his family.

1922   The Soviet Union is formed.

1941   Japanese forces attack the US military base at Pearl Harbor on December 7, drawing the United States into World War II.

1948   North Korea and South Korea are established. Kim Il Sung becomes the leader of North Korea.

1953   The Korean War ends.

Early 1980s   Kim Jong Un is born.

1985   North Korea signs the Nuclear Nonproliferation Treaty.

1991	The Soviet Union collapses.
1994	Kim Il Sung dies, and Kim Jong Il becomes North Korea's leader.
1995–1998	Famine strikes North Korea.
2002	George W. Bush says North Korea is part of an "axis of evil."
2006	North Korea successfully tests a nuclear weapon for the first time.
2011	Kim Jong Il dies, and Kim Jong Un becomes North Korea's supreme leader.
2013	Kim oversees a series of purges, including the execution of his uncle, Jang Song Thaek.
	North Korea tests a nuclear weapon for the first time under the leadership of Kim Jong Un.
2018	Kim and Trump meet in Singapore.

SOURCE NOTES

10   Matthew Pennington and Josh Lederman, "Trump Claim Raises Eyebrows: NKorea No Longer a Nuke Threat?," AP, June 13, 2018, https://www.apnews.com/31b82018ce384e1b99b300e3fbc40cad.

15–16   "Speech by Franklin D. Roosevelt, New York (Transcript)," Library of Congress, accessed June 12, 2018, https://www.loc.gov/resource/afc1986022.afc1986022_ms2201/?st=text&tr=-0.031,-0.101,1.061,0.878,0.

23   Anna Fifield, "The Secret Life of Kim Jong Un's Aunt, Who Has Lived in the U.S. since 1998," *Washington Post*, May 27, 2016, https://www.washingtonpost.com/world/asia_pacific/the-secret-life-of-kim-jong-uns-aunt-who-has-lived-in-the-us-since-1998/2016/05/26/522e4ec8-12d7-11e6-a9b5-bf703a5a7191_story.html?noredirect=on&utm_term=.61973644d59b.

27   "Bush State of the Union Address," *CNN*, January 29, 2002, http://edition.cnn.com/2002/ALLPOLITICS/01/29/bush.speech.txt/.

29   "U.N. Slaps Trade, Travel Sanctions on North Korea," *CNN*, October 15, 2006, http://www.cnn.com/2006/WORLD/asiapcf/10/14/nkorea.sanctions/.

34   Alexander Vorontsov, "North Korea 2012, Grandson Greets Grandfather: Celebration by Satellite Statue," Brookings, April 26, 2012, https://www.brookings.edu/opinions/north-korea-2012-grandson-greets-grandfather-celebration-by-satellite-salute/.

34   "Kim Jong Un Makes First Appearance since Father's Death [Video]," *Los Angeles Times*, December 20, 2011, http://latimesblogs.latimes.com/world_now/2011/12/kim-jong-un-first-appearance.html.

35   "North Korea's Kim Jong-un in First Major Public Speech," *BBC*, April 15, 2012, https://www.bbc.com/news/world-asia-17718011.

36   Tom Watkins, "North Korea Says Leader's Uncle Was Executed," *CNN*, December 12, 2013, https://www.cnn.com/2013/12/12 /world/asia/north-korea-uncle-executed/index.html.

38   Abby Ohlheiser, "North Korea Vows Nuke Tests Will Target U.S., 'Sworn Enemy of the Korean People,'" Slate, January 24, 2013, http://www.slate.com/blogs/the_slatest/2013/01/24/north_korea_ nuclear_tests_kim_jong_un_responds_to_u_n_sanctions_with_ new.html.

40   Noah Bierman, "Trump Warns North Korea of 'Fire and Fury,'" *Los Angeles Times*, August 8, 2017, http://www.latimes.com /politics/washington/la-na-essential-washington-updates-trump -warns-north-korea-of-fire-and-1502220642-htmlstory.html.

40   Philip Rucker, "The 'Dotard' Meets 'Little Rocket Man': Trump and Kim Are Adversaries with Many Similarities," *Washington Post*, June 10, 2018, https://www.washingtonpost.com/politics /the-dotard-meets-little-rocket-man-trump-and-kim-are -adversaries-with-many-similarities/2018/06/09/583b9ddc-6a89 -11e8-bea7-c8eb28bc52b1_story.html?utm_term=.3560a4674609.

40   Rucker.

SELECTED BIBLIOGRAPHY

"Full Text of Trump-Kim Signed Statement." *CNN*, June 12, 2018. https://www.cnn.com/2018/06/12/politics/read-full-text-of-trump-kim-signed-statement/index.html.

"Kim Jong Un Fast Facts." *CNN*, April 30, 2018. https://www.cnn.com/2012/12/26/world/asia/kim-jong-un---fast-facts/index.html.

Lee, Grace. "The Political Philosophy of Juche." *Stanford Journal of East Asia Affairs.* Accessed June 16, 2018. https://s3.amazonaws.com/berkley-center/030101LeePoliticalPhilosophyJuche.pdf.

"North Korea." Amnesty International. Accessed June 16, 2018. https://www.amnesty.org/en/countries/asia-and-the-pacific/north-korea/.

"North Korean Factions." Global Security. Accessed June 16, 2018. https://www.globalsecurity.org/military/world/dprk/leadership-factions.htm.

"North Korea Nuclear." NTI. Accessed June 16, 2018. http://www.nti.org/learn/countries/north-korea/nuclear/.

FURTHER READING

BOOKS

Goldsmith, Connie. *Bombs over Bikini: The World's First Nuclear Disaster.* Minneapolis: Twenty-First Century Books, 2014. Learn about the US government's early experiments with nuclear weapons.

Hall, Kevin, and R. Conrad Stein. *The Korean War.* New York: Enslow, 2017. Find out more about the causes and battles of the Korean War.

Roberts, Russell. *Kim Jong Un: Supreme Leader of North Korea.* Mendota Heights, MN: North Star Editions, 2018. Read more about the life of North Korea's dictator.

WEBSITES

Ducksters—Korea, North
https://www.ducksters.com/geography/country.php?country=Korea,%20North
This website has information about the history, geography, and economy of North Korea.

What Was Kim Jong-un like as a Boy?
https://www.pbs.org/wgbh/frontline/article/what-was-kim-jong-un-like-as-a-boy/
Learn what the world outside of North Korea knows about Kim Jong Un's mysterious childhood.

Why Are North and South Korea Divided?
https://www.history.com/news/north-south-korea-divided-reasons-facts
Explore more of the history of the Korean peninsula.

INDEX